THE REAL UK

Your need-to-know guide for all things British

Paul Mason

FRANKLIN WATTS
LONDON•SYDNEY

Franklin Watts
Published in Great Britain in 2015 by The Watts
Publishing Group

Copyright © The Watts Publishing Group 2013

Series Editor: Sarah Peutrill
Series Designer: Sophie Wilkins
Picture Researcher: Diana Morris

Dewey number: 914.1

ISBN: 978 1 4451 4211 1

Printed in Malaysia

Franklin Watts
An imprint of
Hachette Children's Group
Part of The Watts Publishing Group
Carmelite House
50 Victoria Embankment
London EC4Y 0DZ

An Hachette UK Company
www.hachette.co.uk

www.franklinwatts.co.uk

CONTENTS

● ●

Cotswolds, p. 11

Edinburgh Fringe, p. 31

WHAT'S HOT: UK

Glastonbury fun, p. 28

There is always something to see or do in the UK – whether you want to hike through misty mountains, listen to live music at a festival, watch some of the world's top football teams, tuck into a legendary Cornish pasty or shop at some of the best street markets around.

1. TAKE A BORIS BIKE TOUR OF LONDON p.12

Named after London's eccentric mayor, Boris Johnson, (although they were the previous mayor's idea!) the simple blue bikes are everywhere and are a great way to see the city.

2. HUNT FOR VINTAGE THREADS AT OLD SPITALFIELDS p.14

London is jammed with street markets; this is a great one for vintage clothes, one-off pieces by new designers and ethnic fabrics.

3. EAT A FULL ENGLISH p.18

Few people eat this traditional breakfast every day, but it's a shame not to give it a try. Just don't plan to do anything energetic afterwards!

4. WATCH THE BOAT RACE p.22

One of the oldest and most famous rowing races in the world, the Boat Race was first held in 1829. You can watch free from the banks of the River Thames, or crowd onto Hammersmith Bridge to watch the crews from above. It's also shown live on TV.

Oxford v. Cambridge Boat Race, pp 22–23

5. GET MUDDY AT GLASTONBURY p.28

The UK's biggest and most famous music festival seems to get more than its fair share of rain. It's still fun – but don't forget your wellies.

6. SPEND A WEEKEND IN A TENT p.34

Camping is a great way to experience the UK countryside. In fact, you don't need a tent: you can camp in teepees, treehouses, yurts and all kinds of other oddball shelters.

7. GET ALL STEAMED UP IN DORSET p.36

Every August, steam-powered engines, tractors and other vehicles from around the country converge on north Dorset for the Great Dorset Steam Fair.

8. WATCH THE SUN SET AT CALLANISH p.38

This ancient stone circle on an isolated Scottish island is 4,500 years old – and standing there alone at sunset is as spooky now as it must have been then.

Campsite cricket match, p.34

PUBLIC HOLIDAYS

The UK has national holidays throughout the year; not all are held throughout the UK:

1 January	New Year's Day
2 January	(only in Scotland)
13 March	St Patrick's Day (Northern Ireland only)
Date changes:	Good Friday
Date changes: (England, Northern Ireland, Wales)	Easter Monday
First Monday in May	May Day
Last Monday in May	Spring Holiday
12 July	Orangemen's Day (Northern Ireland)
First Monday in August	Summer Holiday (Scotland)
Last Monday in August	Summer Holiday (England, Northern Ireland, Wales)
30 November	St Andrew's Day (Scotland only)
25 December	Christmas Day
26 December	Boxing Day

UK FACTS AND STATS

Isles of Scilly

The United Kingdom is not very big. In fact, there are 11 US states that are bigger!* But the UK packs a lot into a small space: it contains mountains, ancient monuments, beautiful islands, countryside peppered with thatched cottages and one of the world's most famous cities – London.

*It's smaller than Michigan (no. 11), but bigger than Minnesota (no. 12).

LANDSCAPE

The UK's landscape is mostly hilly. There is flatter land to the south and east, while North Wales and Scotland are mountainous. Landscape highlights to look out for include:

- The UK's tallest mountains in the Highlands of Scotland

- Hills topped with ancient standing stones on the moors of the southwest

- Sandy bays and towering cliffs on the Gower Peninsula, in Wales

- The Giant's Causeway, the remains of an ancient volcanic eruption in Northern Ireland

Key
- ■ Capital city
- ○ Other cities
- ▲ Mountain

Shetland Islands

Orkney Islands

Hebrides

HIGHLANDS
▲ Ben Nevis

SCOTLAND

Glasgow Edinburgh

NORTHERN IRELAND
Belfast

UNITED

CHEVIOT HILLS

North Sea

Newcastle

LAKE DISTRICT

Isle of Man

Bradford

York Hull

REPUBLIC OF IRELAND

Manchester Leeds
Liverpool

KINGDOM Sheffield

River Trent

Irish Sea

ENGLAND River Ouse

CAMBRIAN MOUNTAINS

Birmingham Cambridge
River Severn

WALES

Cardiff Oxford

Bristol Channel Bristol River Thames London

Atlantic Ocean

Isles of Scilly

English Channel

Map of UK

CLIMATE

During winter, the UK's climate is cold enough for everyone to need coats, hats and gloves. In summer on some days, it is warm enough for swimming in the sea (tough people swim in the sea the rest of the year too). Throughout the year, temperatures are likely to be colder further north. Rainclouds can sweep in from the Atlantic Ocean at any time of year, but especially in winter.

WHAT IS THE UNITED KINGDOM?

Four areas make up the United Kingdom:

1. England, Scotland and Wales – occupy the island of Great Britain.

2. Northern Ireland – occupies the northeast part of the island of Ireland.

Confusingly, all citizens – even those from Northern Ireland – are commonly known as 'British' people.

FACT FILE ONE

CAPITAL CITY: London

AREA: 241,930km² of land area, plus 1,680 km² of sea area

HIGHEST MOUNTAIN: Ben Nevis, Scotland (1,343 m)

LOWEST POINT: The Fens (-4 m)

LONGEST RIVER: Severn (354 km)

BORDERS: Northern Ireland borders the Republic of Ireland

NATURAL HAZARDS: flooding, winter storms, blizzards

Ben Nevis

PEOPLE

The UK is a country of immigrants. In ancient times, Roman, Saxon and Norman invaders settled here, and immigrants have been arriving ever since. Recently, more peaceful settlers have come from South Asia, the Caribbean, Eastern Europe, Africa and many other parts of the world. Walk along a busy city street and you can hear the UK's diversity: Polish, Punjabi, Afghan, Australian, Cantonese, Czech, Slovak, Sinhalese and many other languages and accents.

Typical city street scene, Manchester

Typical suburban housing, Bristol

URBAN LIFE

Nearly all of the UK's people live in towns or cities. In city centres, most people live in a flat. Suburbs, where houses are more common, surround most cities. British homes are small compared to some other wealthy countries: on average, US and Australian homes are three times the size, and French homes are 50% bigger.

INTRODUCING UK

RURAL LIFE

Only one in 10 people lives in the countryside. Life in the countryside is more expensive than in towns and cities, because of transport and housing costs. Houses in pretty areas such as the Cotswolds are often bought as holiday homes. Many are empty outside the holiday season, giving some villages a ghost-town vibe.

Quiet Cotswold village

Village maypole dancing

FACT FILE TWO

POPULATION: 63 million

CITIES OF OVER 1 MILLION PEOPLE: London (8.61 million), Birmingham (2.3 million), Manchester (2.25 million), Glasgow (1.17 million)

AGE STRUCTURE: 17.3% under 15 years old; 65.8% 15–64 years old; 16.9% over 64 years old

YOUTH UNEMPLOYMENT (15–24 year-olds): 18.9%

OBESITY: 22.7%

LANGUAGES: English (official language); Scots, Scottish Gaelic, Welsh, Irish and Cornish are official regional languages. After English, Polish and Punjabi are the next most common languages

RELIGIONS: Christians make up 71.6% of the UK population, Muslims 2.7%, Hindus 1%, other religions 1%

LONDON BIKE TOUR

London is one of the world's most influential cities. It is a centre for fashion, art and music – and less interestingly, banking and finance. Ultra-modern buildings stand beside ancient ones from 500 years ago or more. Just wandering around the ancient streets gives you a buzz.

Central London

TAKE A KOOKY 'BORIS BIKE' TOUR

One of the best ways to see London is to pedal your way around on one of the city's 'Boris Bikes'. So, which places could you include on your kooky tour?

The smallest police station, Trafalgar Square, Central London (far right)

This police station is so small, even people who have been to Trafalgar Square probably won't have noticed it. It looks more like a telephone booth than a cop shop.

London catacombs, various locations

During the 1800s, London began to run out of places to put its dead. The answer was to create catacombs – passageways filled with tombs. One of the best is the half-underground one at Highgate Cemetery.

London's oldest inn, Wapping, East London

The Prospect of Whitby (below) has been an inn since the 1500s. It was once so popular with shady characters that it was called The Devil's Tavern. After a fire in the 1800s, the inn was renamed in the hope of attracting a better class of customer.

The Cathedral of Sewage, Newham, East London

'Cathedral of Sewage' is actually a nickname – this building's real name is Abbey Mills Pumping Station. It's one of the few parts of London's Victorian sewage system you can visit, though the tours only happen once a year (usually in May).

Ancient inn beside the Thames

BORIS BIKES

Boris Bikes are nicknamed after Mayor Boris Johnson. They can be hired at 'docking stations' (right) around London. You pay a small fee for access to the docking stations. After that, up to half an hour's bike use is free.

London's smallest police station

LONDON MYTHS

MYTH: There's a street lamp in Carting Lane that runs on sewer gas from the Savoy Hotel

Some London gas lamps once did run partly on sewer gas – but not any more. The one on Carting Lane is a replica of those old-style gas lamps.

MYTH: When the Union flag is flying over Buckingham Palace, the Queen is home

Actually, it means she's out. When Her Majesty is there, the Royal Standard will be flying.

MYTH: There are no 'Roads' in the City of London

People will often tell you that the City (the old Square Mile at the very heart of London) contains no routes called 'Road'. They're nearly correct – but since 1994, Goswell Road has technically been half in the City.

LONDON: FASHION CITY

London is the fashion capital of the UK, and one of the world's leading cities for clothing design. In fact, in 2012 London was voted the world's MOST fashionable city. Spend an hour or two in the coolest parts of town, and you're bound to see someone walk past wearing next year's look.

CAMDEN TOWN

Camden is a centre for London's underground music scene: head here to see what the well-dressed groover is wearing this year. At Camden Market you'll find a maze of tiny stalls selling all kinds of clothing and other products.

Haringay

Islington

Hackney

Camden

Tower Hamlets

NOTTING HILL

This is where you'll find one of London's most famous street markets, on Portobello Road. The mile-long stretch of stalls sells different kinds of goods on different days: go on a Friday or Saturday for clothes.

SPITALFIELDS

Spitalfields ranges from the Bangladeshi community of Brick Lane to the towering office buildings of the City. At its heart is Old Spitalfields Market, which is great for one-off designer items, vintage clothing and fabrics.

THE CAPITAL

"You have a much better life if you wear impressive clothes."

— UK fashion designer Vivienne Westwood

HOXTON

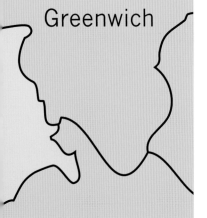

The unofficial coolest neighbourhood in London, Hoxton is a great place for trend spotting. You'll laugh at the ridiculous fashions and haircuts – only to find yourself copying them in six months' time.

Greenwich

LONDON FASHION WEEK

London Fashion Week is one of the world's biggest fashion events (the others are in New York, Paris and Milan). It is held twice a year, in February and September. Catwalk shows display designers' clothes for the next season.

It's basically impossible for ordinary people to get tickets, but some shows are now streamed live on the Internet.

BUCKINGHAM PALACE AND ROYAL BRITAIN

Royal wedding fever, April 2011

For the wedding of Prince William and Kate Middleton in 2011, and the 2012 Queen's Jubilee, everyone in the UK was given an extra day off work. They celebrated by wearing fancy dress, holding street parties and generally having a good time. No wonder the Royal Family is so popular!

BUCKINGHAM PALACE

You can't really visit London without a trip to Buckingham Palace. This has been the official home of the British monarch since 1837, when Queen Victoria saw its potential as a fixer-upper and moved in.

These days, millions of people visit Buckingham Palace each year. Mainly they have their photo taken outside, next to the unflinching, unsmiling Guardsmen. But the Queen's Gallery, where her art collection is displayed, is open to the public. It is also possible to visit the State Rooms during July and August.

> "I am glad we have been bombed. Now I can look the East End in the face."
>
> — Queen Elizabeth, wife of King George VI, after Buckingham Palace was bombed in 1940. The East End had already been hit by German bombers, and large areas destroyed.

Buckingham Palace parade

A BRITISH STREET PARTY

How do you organise a British street party?
1. Ask the police for permission to close your street.
2. Set out long tables, chairs and Union Jack bunting.
3. Ask all your neighbours to bring food and drink: typically sandwiches, cakes, tea and squash.
4. Hope it doesn't rain!

Traditional street party

OTHER ROYAL RESIDENCES

Buckingham Palace is not the Queen's only residence. Others include:

1. Sandringham House, Norfolk, England – Though it looks very old-fashioned now, Sandringham was once cutting edge. It had gas lamps, flushing toilets and even a shower when these things were very unusual. It is possible to visit the grounds and house at certain times of the year.

2. Balmoral Castle, Aberdeenshire, Scotland – Built for Queen Victoria in 1856, Balmoral's gardens are open to visitors from April to the end of July. It is also possible to visit the grand ballroom.

3. Windsor Castle, Berkshire, England – The original castle was built in the 11th century. It was used as a refuge for the Royal Family during air raids in the Second World War (1939–45) and survived a fire in 1992. The Queen likes to spend her weekends here.

FOOD AND EATING

Most British people eat three meals a day: breakfast, lunch and dinner. Many also snack throughout the day – which might be why one in five of them are now dangerously overweight. People in the UK have an amazingly varied menu, which includes dishes from all round the world.

In the past, British food had a terrible reputation. People said that it was usually frozen, deep-fried or boiled to tastelessness – and they were mostly correct. These days, though, most British people prefer fresh ingredients cooked in a tasty, healthy way.

TYPICAL FOODS

These are a few typical UK dishes. Note that this isn't a typical day's eating – if you ate all these suggestions, you'd burst!

Breakfast (eaten between 07:30-09:30)

Most people have cereal or toast, with tea to drink. Every visitor to the UK should try the 'full English' breakfast once, though. This typically contains toast or fried bread, egg, bacon, sausage, mushrooms, baked beans, fried potato, black pudding and tomato. There are regional variations: full Scottish and Welsh breakfasts, and the 'Ulster fry'.

Lunch (eaten between 12:30-14:30)

Most adults eat a sandwich for lunch. Schools offer students a choice of food which usually includes salads, pasta and rice dishes. A weekend favourite is a Sunday roast, which is roast meat, roast potatoes, gravy and vegetables.

Classic fried breakfast

Dinner, Tea or Supper

(eaten between 18:00-20:30)

Dinnertime really shows off the UK's multicultural history. In a typical week people might eat cottage pie, Thai curry, stir-fried meat and vegetables, spaghetti Bolognese, chicken curry and pizza.

> **"It takes some skill to spoil a breakfast – even the English can't do it."**
>
> — (American) economist JK Galbraith

WHAT'S IN A NAME?

In some areas of the UK, people call their meal in the middle of the day 'dinner', rather than 'lunch'. The evening meal is then known as 'tea'. Another term, 'supper', is used all over the UK. It may describe a light meal or snack that is eaten late at night – although for some it may be what they call the evening meal.

Sunday roast

THE UK'S TOP 10 MEALS

This list of the UK's 10 favourite family meals appeared in 2009:

1. Spaghetti Bolognese
2. Sunday roast
3. Chilli con carne
4. Lasagne
5. Cottage/shepherd's pie (cottage pie is made with beef, shepherd's pie with lamb)
6. Chinese stir fry
7. Beef stew
8. Macaroni cheese
9. Toad in the hole (sausages baked in batter)
10. Curry

FOOTBALL AND THE FA CUP

Britain's favourite sport by far is football. The modern game was invented in Britain, then exported around the world. Sadly, the rest of the world soon got quite a lot better at it than the British. That hasn't stopped people loving football, though!

Football at a local sports ground

STREET FOOTBALL

You see street football being played everywhere in the UK. Any bit of waste ground, park or empty basketball court will probably have kids playing on it. Street football games normally use one 'goal' (which is often two piles of sweatshirts, or a space on a wall) and only need three players.

LEAGUE FOOTBALL

Most places in the UK have a proper 11-a-side football team, even small villages. As a result, on weekends during the season (August–May) you're never far from a game to watch. The sport is governed by the Football Association (FA), which organises leagues and other competitions.

"Some people believe football's a matter of life and death. I'm very disappointed with that attitude. I can assure you it's much more important than that."

— famous football manager Bill Shankly

THE FA CUP'S BIGGEST SHOCKS

1972: Hereford v. Newcastle
Newcastle are one of the country's top teams. Hereford don't even play in one of the top four divisions – but they still win 2–1. It is the biggest upset in FA Cup history.

1984: Bournemouth v. Manchester United
United are the UK's top team, and have won the Cup more times than anyone else. But they still get beaten 2–0 by Third Division (now called League One) Bournemouth.

The FA Cup

SPORT

THE FA CUP

The oldest football competition of all is the FA Cup. This is one of those sports events that even people who aren't interested in sport like to watch. Teams are drawn randomly to decide who plays one another. Some of the Cup's most exciting stories happen when a small team beats a bigger one. If you buy a ticket to one of the early rounds, you might even see a surprise result.

Wigan beat Manchester City in the 2013 FA Cup final

BIG UK EVENTS

Grand National winner on parade

Rugby fans, Six Nations

Since London held the Olympic Games in 2012, the UK has been swept with enthusiasm for sport. The streets are full of people jogging, cycling or on their way to the gym, and it is difficult to get a ticket for any of the country's big sports events.

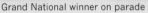

Boat Race crowds, Hammersmith Bridge

SPORTS DIARY OF THE YEAR

When these happen, the streets are noticeably quiet – until something exciting happens, when you hear the shouts and cheers coming out of people's windows!

FEBRUARY– MARCH:

Six Nations rugby

The Six Nations are England, France, Ireland, Italy, Scotland and Wales. Watching it on TV is fun – but if you can get tickets it's even more exciting. If you can, go to a match on the final day: the top team is usually decided then, so these are nerve-shredding games for the fans.

MARCH OR APRIL:

The Boat Race

The top rowers of Oxford and Cambridge universities battle it out over 6.8 km of the River Thames. It's free to watch from the bank, though it might be hard to find a space. About 250,000 people turned up in 2013 – and millions more watched on TV.

APRIL:

Grand National

The UK's most popular horse race is so popular that the government decided the race has to be shown free, on a TV channel everyone can access. First held in 1839, the Grand National is today watched by over 500 million people, in 140 different countries.

MAY:

FA Cup final, football

See page 21 for more information about the FA Cup.

JUNE–JULY:

Wimbledon

The Wimbledon Championships is the biggest tennis tournament in the world, the one every player dreams of winning. If you can't afford courtside tickets, don't panic: the hillside at Aorangi Terrace has a giant screen showing the big matches live.

OTHER EVENTS TO LOOK OUT FOR

These sports events do not happen every year, but when they're on, sports fans get excited:

The Ashes (cricket tournament between England and Australia every two years)

The Ryder Cup (Europe v. USA golf contest, held every two years)

Commonwealth Games (athletics event every four years: hosted by the Scottish city of Glasgow in 2014)

SPORT

STREET SPORTS AND TRADITIONAL GAMES

Street sports and the UK's traditional games may not at first seem to have much in common. Both, though, often have an anarchic, slightly disorganised character. The lack of rules, regulations and referees is especially appealing to the UK's young people.

Skateboarders, Brighton sea front

STREET SPORTS

Since most people in the UK live in cities, the appeal of sports you can do in any kind of urban environment is obvious.

Skateboarding
Most towns and cities have a skate park of some sort, and taking your skateboard to the local park is a good way to meet people.

BMX
BMX is one of the UK's most popular street sports, and some of the world's best riders are British: riders such as Danny MacAskill, Mike Mullen and Bas Keep.

Parkour/free running
Ever since the Bond film *Casino Royale* opened with a breathtaking parkour sequence, the activity of moving yourself forward using any object around you has become increasingly popular in the UK. Towns and cities with active parkour scenes include Glasgow, Manchester, Nottingham, Norwich, Aberystwyth, London and Exeter.

"Parkour is getting over all the obstacles in your path as you would in an emergency situation."

— David Belle, one of the founders of parkour

TRADITIONAL GAMES

Traditional games from hundreds of years ago are still popular in the UK. Here are three:

The Ba Game (Scotland)
The Ba Game is a kind of rugby-football mash-up played between large groups. It can be hours before a goal (which wins the contest) is scored.

Tug-of-war
Two teams take hold of opposite ends of a rope. Each tries to pull the other forward. Put a river or stream between them, and it gets really interesting.

Cheese rolling (Gloucestershire)
People carrying large, round cheeses climb a steep hill. Then they roll their cheese down, following behind as fast as possible. First cheese and person to the bottom wins. Unsurprisingly the event is known for injuries to those taking part (and even the spectators), with sprains and broken bones being common.

SPORT

Airborne Ba Game player

Cheese rollers in action

MUSIC

From rap to dance, pop, and folk, the UK has a thriving music scene. New bands spring up and disappear all the time. Most big towns have venues where you can see live music, ranging from small rooms that will hold 40 or 50 people to giant stadiums.

Harbour Festival in Bristol

THE BRITISH MUSIC EXPERIENCE

The British Music Experience in Greenwich, London is a great place to visit if you're into music. The museum has a rolling programme of exhibits about British music since 1945. You can see photos and videos of top bands, walk along the Sound Tunnel, gawp at old Spice Girls outfits, flick through the virtual collection of 12" singles in the Hey DJ! experience, and much more.

MUSIC FROM AROUND THE WORLD

The UK has been welcoming immigrants for centuries, and the new arrivals brought their music with them. As a result you can hear just about any kind of music imaginable on the UK's streets, from calypso to choral singing, didgeridoo playing, drumming and ukulele music.

MUSIC TO LISTEN OUT FOR

What are you most likely to hear coming from radios, being played in cafés, or live on stage in the UK? The most popular types of music include:

Rock:
the biggest UK bands include Coldplay and the wonderfully named British Sea Power; Mumford & Sons are a huge folk rock band.

Pop:
dominated by female singers, including Adele and Jessie J.

R&B:
foreign acts such as Rihanna and Nicki Minaj get a lot of radio play.

Rap and hip-hop:
British talents include Dizzee Rascal and Tinie Tempah.

Dance:
Scotland's Calvin Harris and Frenchman David Guetta are among the top DJ/producers.

● ●

> "I make music for the hips, not the head."
>
> — Norman Cook, a.k.a. top British DJ Fatboy Slim

THE X-FACTOR

If you are in the UK between September and December, expect to hear people talking about *The X-Factor*. This TV show is a music competition that aims to find the most promising new act each year. *The X Factor* has been wildly popular since it began in 2004.

CULTURE

Pop fans at the O2 Arena, one of the largest venues in Europe

GLASTONBURY FESTIVAL

Glastonbury is Britain's biggest music festival, and one of the most famous in the world. This monster of an event happens almost every year, on the weekend in June closest to the longest day in the year. It is held on a farm in Somerset, in the south west of England.

Glastonbury is not a festival where you can turn up on the day and pay to get in. The 2013 event sold out all 135,000 tickets within two hours. If you ARE lucky enough to get a ticket, you'll hear all kinds of music inside the fence that surrounds the site, from rock to rap, R&B and dance.

Glastonbury mudfest

GLASTONBURY SURVIVAL KIT CHECKLIST

There are a LOT of people at Glastonbury – and being the UK, it's quite likely to be rainy. What do you need to survive?

Wellington boots
Wellies are the only way to keep your feet dry and clean if the ground gets muddy.

Flag on a pole
Put this up beside your tent, so that you can find your tent among the thousands of other similar ones.

Earplugs
Because even the biggest music fan has to sleep at some point!

OTHER MUSIC FESTIVALS

You could spend a very happy musical summer visiting festivals across the UK. There are over 300 each year. Here are four:

MAY:

Evolution
(Newcastle, England)

Held on three sites beside the River Tyne, Evolution is mostly dance and electronic music, with some hip-hop and pop.

JUNE:

Isle of Wight Festival
(Isle of Wight, England)

The grand old daddy of music festivals, this got so big and troublesome that in 1970 an Act of Parliament banned it! The festival restarted in 2002 and has been going ever since.

JULY:

T in the Park
(Kinross-shire, Scotland)

Rock, pop and dance all mixed together on a disused airfield outside the town of Kinross.

AUGUST:

Reading Festival
(Berkshire, England)

Mostly heavy metal, rock and pop, but with some dance and other music thrown in.

CULTURE

FOUNDING THE GLASTONBURY FESTIVAL

In 1970, a farmer and music fan called Michael Eavis decided to build a stage at his farm near Glastonbury, and invite bands to come and play. Everyone – festivalgoers and musicians – could camp in the fields. From the start Glastonbury attracted top acts: the first headliners were T-Rex, followed in 1971 by David Bowie.

Smaller, 1970s Glastonbury Festival

EDINBURGH FESTIVAL

At Edinburgh Festival, you never know what's round the corner

The Edinburgh Fringe is said to be the biggest arts festival in the world. It specialises in comedy and theatre, but you can also see cutting-edge dance and music. In 2012, the Fringe lasted 25 days, during which there were 2,695 shows. Put another way, that's almost five shows an hour, every hour, all day and night.

WHAT TO SEE?

With so many performances, it can be a bit tricky to work out what you want to see. One good place for information is the pedestrian area around St Giles' Cathedral. Here, performers hand out flyers, and sometimes perform excerpts from their show as a taster.

"You know who really gives kids a bad name? Posh and Becks."

— unofficial best joke at the 2012 Edinburgh Festival, by comedian Stewart Francis

OTHER EDINBURGH FESTIVAL EVENTS

The Fringe is not the only festival based in Edinburgh. Here are three of the others (two of which also happen in August):

Edinburgh International Festival

This was started after the Second World War, to promote the 'flowering of the human spirit' after five years of conflict. It features classical music, theatre and dance: something to occupy your parents, perhaps?

Royal Edinburgh Military Tattoo

If you like the idea of sitting in an old castle watching marching bands and people dragging guns back and forth, the Military Tattoo is for you. It is so popular that it's said to be televised in 30 countries and is watched by 100 million people each year.

Edinburgh International Film Festival

The world's oldest continuously running film festival, EIFF used to happen in August alongside the rest of the Festival. It now takes place in June.

Street theatre, Edinburgh Fringe performers

The Royal Edinburgh Military Tattoo

HOLIDAYS

The UK is a great place to take a holiday. It's so small that four days is long enough for a trip to almost anywhere. Whether you want cities, countryside, beaches or mountains, it's all within reach!

A VISIT TO THE SOUTHWEST

One of the most popular holidays in the UK is a visit to the southwest of England. Here are a few questions you'll need to ask yourself before your trip:

Beaches or moors?

Do you want to surf the Atlantic waves of the north coast? Or would you rather walk on the inland moors, hunting for ancient standing stones?

Camping or a roof over your head?

There are campsites everywhere (see pages 34–35). You can also stay in a teepee, a treehouse or a shiny-steel American caravan. If you prefer to sleep indoors, there are plenty of 'Bed and Breakfasts' (B&Bs) and hotels.

Self-catering or not?

During the summer, campsites are filled with the smell of barbecues. But if you don't want to cook your own food, try a take-away pasty – a pastry parcel filled with meat and vegetables.

Newquay beach, Cornwall

Unusual hotel accommodation

HOLIDAY HOTSPOTS IN THE UK

LAKE DISTRICT
First popular in the Victorian era, the Lakes (and the surrounding mountains) are still a favourite destination.

HIGHLANDS AND ISLANDS
Visit the UK's tallest mountains, then continue the adventure by ferry-hopping between islands off the coast.

YORKSHIRE DALES
Known for breathtaking walking and cycling routes on the hills, and pretty villages hidden in the valleys.

NORTHERN IRELAND BEACHES
A well-kept secret, these are popular with surfers, walkers and (when possible) sunbathers.

THE BROADS
A boating holiday destination, the area also attracts ramblers, artists, anglers and bird-watchers.

SOUTHWEST WALES
The Gower Peninsula and Pembrokeshire each have beautiful sandy beaches and countryside.

SOUTHWEST ENGLAND
Also called the West Country – see **Visit to the southwest** on page 32 for details.

CAMPING BRITAIN

Campside cricket match

In the last 10 years the number of campers in the UK has grown massively. Some go camping for a weekend away from the city, others for a family holiday near the beach. Whatever the reason, the UK's campsites have never been busier.

WHERE CAN YOU CAMP?

In England, Wales and Northern Ireland, you are only really allowed to camp on an official campsite. These range from big sites with swimming pools, entertainment centres and laundries, to farmers' fields with a toilet in the corner. Some even offer 'glamping' (short for 'glamorous camping').

In Scotland, things are different. You can camp practically anywhere! The only rules for 'wild camping' are:

- Avoid farmland, whether for animals or crops
- Camp well away from buildings, ancient monuments and roads
- Don't stay more than three nights in one place
- Take your rubbish away with you
- Leave the camping spot as you found it

Camping at Three Cliffs Bay, Wales

ART OF THE BARBECUE: 3 STEPS TO BARBECUE HEAVEN.

1. Place your barbecue on something that a) doesn't wobble and b) won't catch light.

2. Use firelighters and wait until the coals are white before putting on your food.

3. Check that the food is cooked right through before you eat it.

CAMPING SURVIVAL CHECKLIST

LEISURE

Camping is great fun as long as you're warm, dry and comfortable. This checklist will make sure you are!

 Tent
A tent with an inner and outer layer is best. Pitch your tent on level ground and peg it out so that the sides don't flap.

 Sleeping bag
Pick a 2-season bag for warm weather, a 3- or 4-season if it's colder.

Sleep mat and pillow
Having these will make sure you have a good night's sleep.

 Hat and fleece
If you get cold at night, putting on a hat is a great way to warm up.

 Wellies or flip-flops
Shoes you can take on and off quickly before getting in the tent.

COUNTRY FAIRS

If there's one event that is typically British, it's a summer fair. Many of these are enormous, with funfairs and row after row of stalls selling products and all sorts of food. In fact, you might find it hard to believe that some fairs are hundreds of years old.

Holkham Country Fair, Norfolk

Great Dorset Steam Fair action

THE GREAT DORSET STEAM FAIR

If you are interested in steam-powered anything, head for north Dorset in August. The Great Dorset Steam Fair's most popular attractions include tractors, traction engines and farm machinery. But there's also a steam-powered funfair, classic cars and motorbikes, and working heavy horses to see. Just be sure to leave plenty of time for your journey. The roads will be clogged with owners driving their steam-powered vehicles to and from the show. Some of these only do about 15 kph, so they can be overtaken on a bicycle!

ON THE MENU AT THE FAIR

If you stumble on a small village fair, there will almost certainly be a choice of traditional fair-time food. Take your pick from:

- Sponge cakes
- Cucumber or cheese-and-tomato sandwiches
- Tea or lemonade

OTHER OUTDOOR EVENTS

The Great Dorset Steam Fair may be the biggest, but it's not the only outdoor event. Here are two more oddball choices:

Appleby Horse Fair
(Cumbria, England)

Since 1685, Gypsies from across the British Isles have been coming to Appleby. They head here every June, to buy and sell horses and to meet with relatives and friends. There is a similar fair eight weeks later in Brough, Cumbria.

Whitstable Oyster Festival
(Kent, England)

There has been an oyster festival in Whitstable ever since the Romans started tucking into the local shellfish. It takes place every July. If you don't like oysters, look out for the belly-dancing lessons and Blessing of the Sea ceremony.

Trotting through the streets of Appleby

LEISURE

VISIT ANCIENT BRITAIN

The UK is littered with traces of the ancient peoples who lived there thousands of years ago. They are most common in the western regions: England's southwest, Wales, western Scotland and Northern Ireland. These places were occupied tens of thousands of years ago by Celtic tribes.

Stonehenge

STONE CIRCLES TO VISIT

Arriving at either of these lonely places at dawn or sunset makes it easy to imagine what they must have been like thousands of years ago:

Stonehenge, Wiltshire, England

The UK's most famous stone circle is on Salisbury Plain, a high, flat area of land that stretches into the distance.

Callanish, Isle of Lewis, Scotland

A local legend says that these stones are the remains of giants, who were turned to stone as a punishment for not becoming Christians – however, the stones pre-date Christianity.

STONE CIRCLES AND STANDING STONES

There are hundreds of ancient standing stones in the UK, many of them visible from a car or train window. Some are arranged into stone circles, while others stand alone, often on lonely hilltops. Many circles are associated with strange legends. The Merry Maidens in Cornwall are said to be the remnants of local girls turned to stone for dancing on a Sunday. One of the giant stones at Avebury in Wiltshire is said to cross the road at midnight. And chipping bits off the Rollright Stones apparently brings down a deadly curse on your head.

HILL FORTS

There are ancient hill forts, where ancient people cut terraces into the hillsides and built defences, all around the UK. There are over 3,000 in total. You're most likely to see them in southwest England, the west coasts of Wales and Scotland, and in the border areas between England, Scotland and Wales. Walking up to one of these and imagining yourself as someone from the ancient world is a great way to spend an hour or two.

HILL FORTS TO VISIT

Pen Dynas, Ceredigion, Wales

Overlooking the sea, and with rivers on two sides, Pen Dynas is one of the biggest hill forts in Wales.

Yeavering Bell, Northumberland, England

This would have been a hill fort with a difference, because its walls are made of a local stone that starts life pink! These days the colour has faded to dull grey.

Maiden Castle, Dorset, England

Among the largest and most complex of Iron Age hill forts in Europe.

THE CULT OF MITHRAS

The Romans brought the Cult of Mithras to Britain. Little is known about the Cult, but it was associated with the military. We know that members met in caverns or underground halls, and sacrificed bulls to the god. Secret Roman temples of Mithras have been discovered underground. At Temple Court, London, one of these is open to visitors.

Maiden Castle Iron Age hill fort, Dorchester, Dorset

LEISURE

NORTHERN IRELAND

Northern Ireland beach and countryside

Northern Ireland is the only part of the UK that isn't on the island of Great Britain. Instead, it shares the island of Ireland with the Republic of Ireland. It is an increasingly popular place to visit.

PROTESTANT AND CATHOLIC

Northern Ireland has two main communities, based on people's religion. The first is the Protestants, who mostly think it is important for Northern Ireland to be part of the UK. The second community is the Catholics, many of whom think Northern Ireland ought to be part of the Republic of Ireland. In the past, arguments over this subject have become violent.

Until recently, this violence has kept visitors away. These days the communities live more peacefully and more visitors come to the area. Northern Ireland's key attractions are its scenery, heritage and sporting activities.

Wall mural, Belfast

1922: THE DIVISION OF IRELAND

For generations before 1922, the island of Ireland was part of the UK. After years of protests by Irish people, most of the island became an independent country in 1922. Only the northeast corner was kept as part of the UK.

THE *CRAIC*

In Ireland you often hear people talking about 'the *craic*' (pronounced 'crack'). There's no direct translation for this word, but it means a good time, something that's a lot of fun.

TOP ATTRACTIONS

This insider guide will give you some ideas for a visit to Northern Ireland:

Walk on the Giant's Causeway

Thousands of rock pillars, which look as if they have been carved, are actually the result of an ancient volcanic eruption.

Hide yourself away at Binders Cove

Over a thousand years ago, this underground passageway was built to hide people and treasures from Viking raiders.

Take a black-taxi tour of Belfast

Black cabs are a traditional way to get around, and some offer tours of the city. Keep a special eye out for Belfast's colourful wall murals.

Check out St George's Market, Belfast

This old covered market is somewhere to pick up anything from buttons to shoes, lampshades or even shark meat.

The Giant's Causeway

AWAY FROM THE MAINLAND

KEY INFORMATION
FOR TRAVELLERS

LANGUAGE

English is spoken everywhere. The Welsh language had almost disappeared by the 1980s, but has been brought back to life and is now widely spoken in Wales. In Scotland and Northern Ireland, Gaelic is sometimes spoken.

ENTERING THE UK

People from European Union countries can enter the UK without a visa, though arrivals at airports and ferry ports usually have to show their passport.

Visitors from other countries may need a visa, so it is important to check with your own government whether this is required.

GETTING AROUND

The UK has a good railway system connecting its cities and towns, though trains can be expensive unless tickets are booked in advance (see www.nationalrail.co.uk). Buses run in large cities and towns, though in rural areas they may not appear often, if at all. Cycling is a good way to travel short distances, but only folding bikes can be taken on busy trains.

Red London double-decker buses are famous around the world

HEALTH

If you have a minor health problem such as a sore throat, a pharmacy could be a good source of help.

Almost everyone who needs to see a doctor in Britain uses the National Health Service. Emergency treatment is free, but visitors from other countries usually have to pay for non-emergency medical help.

POSTAL SERVICES

The main postal service in the UK is provided by the Post Office. You can buy stamps at post offices and at many other shops: newsagents are a likely place to buy them.

Letters can be posted in the red post boxes that are a common sight on street corners. Parcels have to be taken to a post office for posting. Use first class mail for urgent post as second class mail takes a few days. International mail will take even longer.

MOBILE NETWORKS

The main European mobile-phone networks are all available in the UK. Using a foreign phone – even on the same network as you have at home – is expensive, especially for data, so it's important to turn off data roaming unless you have a UK SIM card. (If you are visiting the UK for a long time, it is easy and inexpensive to buy a SIM with a monthly unlimited-data payment.)

INTERNET PROVISION

The UK generally has excellent Internet provision. Free wifi zones are available in many public spaces, hotels and cafés. Cybercafés offer paid Internet access and computer use, and public libraries often offer the same thing free or for a small charge.

Typical post box

CURRENCY:

Pound (£1 = roughly €1.18, or $1.5). Currency exchange is available at larger banks, bureau de change, post offices, some department stores and train stations.

TIME ZONE:

Greenwich Mean Time (GMT)

On the last Sunday in March, the UK switches to British Summer Time and clocks are put forward one hour. On the last Sunday in October clocks are put back to GMT.

TELEPHONE DIALLING CODES:

To call the UK from outside the country, add 44 to the beginning of the number, and drop the zero.

To call another country from the UK, add OO and the country code of the place you are dialling to the beginning of the number, and drop the zero.

OPENING HOURS:

In cities and towns, most shops are open by 10:00 and closed by 19:00 from Monday to Saturday. On Sundays, they are usually open between 11:00 and 16:00. Some shops open for much longer, for example from 07:00 to 23:00, and a few stay open 24 hours a day, 7 days a week.

In the countryside, shops are generally open 09:00–18:00, but may be closed on Saturday and Wednesday afternoons, and all day on Sunday.

DECIPHERING ENGLISH:

British people don't always mean what they seem to mean – in fact, sometimes they mean the opposite. Here are a few English phrases that can trip up visitors:

English person says:	Visitor hears:	Actual meaning:
Quite good.	Quite good.	Not very good.
It's probably my fault...	He thinks it's his fault.	It's not my fault. It's yours.
With respect...	I respect you.	I have no respect for you.
Of course, you do have other options.	You have a choice.	Your current choice is stupid.

FINDING OUT MORE

BOOKS TO READ: NON-FICTION

The Smell of Poo Closed Parliament! The Fact or Fiction behind London Adam Sutherland (Wayland, 2012)
Part of an excellent series exploring the truth (or otherwise) behind common myths, this is a great, fun-filled read about London. There's a second history title called *Medieval People Washed Their Clothes In Wee* by Kay Barnham.

London: A Time Traveller's Guide Moira Butterfield (Franklin Watts, 2013)
Imagine you could step into a time machine and travel through the centuries to discover some of London's hidden secrets. This book takes you on an incredible trip through London's amazing story.

BOOKS TO READ: FICTION

Goodnight Mr Tom
Michelle Margorian
When Willie Beech is evacuated to the countryside during the Second World War, he is a sad, damaged boy. But Willie slowly works his way to a better place with the help of his host, old Tom Oakley.

Stoneheart Trilogy
Charlie Fletcher (Hodder)
The trilogy, set in the streets of London, follows George and Edie, as they struggle to repair the damage George has done at the start of the story by breaking a stone dragon statue.

The Story of Tracey Beaker
Jacqueline Wilson
The 'autobiography' of Tracey Beaker, rebel and resident of The Dumping Ground – a children's home from which Tracey dreams of one day being rescued by her glamorous mother.

WEBSITES

http://www.visitbritain.com
This is a government-backed site. It is aimed not only at people who want to visit Britain, but also British people who would like to see a new part of the country. It is packed with information, but the most useful sections are probably 'Things to do' and 'Destinations and maps'.

There are individual sites for each of the four areas that make up the UK:
www.visitengland.org,
www.visitscotland.co.uk,
www.visitwales.com
www.discovernorthernireland.com.

https://www.cia.gov/library/publications/the-world-factbook/geos/uk.html
This link will take you to the CIA (Central Intelligence Agency) web page about the United Kingdom. It's quite dry, but crammed full of useful information and statistics.

Note to parents and teachers:
Every effort has been made by the Publishers to ensure that these websites are suitable for children, that they are of the highest educational value, and that they contain no inappropriate or offensive material. However, because of the nature of the Internet, it is impossible to guarantee that the contents of these sites will not be altered. We strongly advise that Internet access is supervised by a responsible adult.

THE ESSENTIALS

INDEX